PROJECT

PROJECT

Countering Civil Rights

Tony Bunyan

Tony Bunyan, editor of Statewatch, scrutinises the emerging 'counter-terrorism' regime of the G8 countries and the European Union, in which 'exceptional and draconian' measures are becoming the norm. His report forms a keynote text for the 2005 Conference of the European Network for Peace and Human Rights, which meets in the European Parliament in Brussels on 20/21 October (see www.russfound.org). Updates to the text will be posted at www.statewatch.org.

The United Kingdom government has replaced powers to detain suspected terrorists under the Anti-Terrorism, Crime and Security Act 2001 (ATCSA 2001) with the Prevention of Terrorism Act 2005 (PTA 2005, see Part 2).

In place of indefinite detention in Belmarsh prison, the Prevention of Terrorism Act 2005 has introduced 'control orders' which will be based on 'intelligence assessments' prepared by MI5 and authorised by the Home Secretary. 'Control orders' include 'tagging', no mobile phones or internet access, restricted movements, and indefinite 'house arrests'. Individuals will be able to appeal against the orders and conditions, but these judicial hearings will effectively take place *in camera* without the defendant or their lawyers being present.

Those who were held in Belmarsh have now all been released and put on 'control orders'. People put under 'control orders' will not be charged with a criminal offence and brought before a court and will not know the evidence against them.

The United Kingdom derogated from Article 5 of the European Convention on Human Rights – the only European Union state do so – under Part IV of the Anti-Terrorism, Crime and Security Act 2001. 'House arrests' under the new Act means it will have to derogate again. Such a derogation is only allowed where there is a 'public emergency threatening the life of the nation'. The government claims that the country is living under a permanent 'state of emergency' threatening the 'life of the nation'.

However, what is happening in the United Kingdom is indicative of other, wider developments. Behind the scenes in G8 (comprising the United States, Britain, France, Germany, Italy, Canada, Japan, Russia plus the European Union) the Council of the European Union, and the Council of Europe far-reaching changes are being planned. The first is to broaden 'terrorist offences' to cover preparatory and associated acts, even where no terrorist attack has been carried out, or even planned, and for *apologie*, condoning or sympathising with terrorism.

Second, within these broader remits, to make lawful the use of 'special investigative techniques', such as tapping, bugging, informers, bribes, undercover agents, access to all government databases (data-mining) and the sharing of this 'intelligence' with other agencies – whether inside or outside the European Union. Where 'obstacles' exist, such as requiring judicial authorisation, these should be overcome. 'Self regulation' by the agencies, with all the dangers of misuse and abuse, is to be the new norm.

Third, the intelligence gathered should be used in court while ensuring that it is 'protected'. The 'protection' of intelligence will inevitably be counter to the normal rule of law and the rights of defendants in a democracy.

The inexorable build up of 'intelligence' is fuelling these demands for new offences where people cannot now be charged and brought before the courts. The intelligence products gathered by the use of a wide range of 'special investigative techniques' will be 'protected' in court – so that the defendant will never know what the evidence is against them, where it came from, and how it was gathered.

The United States and the United Kingdom invaded Iraq together. The United States and the United Kingdom have detained people indefinitely without trial and in defiance of the rule of law. Now in a classic case of 'policy-laundering' the United States, backed by the United Kingdom, is working through the G8 group of countries to get these demands agreed in the European Union. Indeed they have offered to draw up a list of 'obstacles' to 'compliance' with them for European Union member states to overcome.

These new offences, techniques and changes in the legal process are likely to spill over into the mainstream criminal justice system and establish new norms – the discussion refers to transnational crime and crime in general. For example, nowhere is it suggested that the use of 'special investigative techniques' should be limited to tackling terrorism; 'terrorism' is simply grounds on which to legitimate their usage. What has been seen as exceptional and draconian becomes the norm.[1]

Using public and secret documents, this report looks at moves in the United Kingdom, United States, the G8, the Council of the European Union, and the Council of Europe to introduce new, preparatory offences including *apologie*, 'intelligence information' as 'evidence' in court gathered by 'special investigative techniques' including from third states, and asks can the rule of law and democratic standards survive?

United Kingdom: From 'spin' to 'control orders'

Former Home Secretary, David Blunkett, while in India, announced proposals on 1 February 2004. He said that where 'suspected' terrorists were concerned, the government wanted to take pre-emptive action by lowering the standard of proof so that suspects could be arrested and charged before mounting an attack, and for them to be tried in secret (*in camera*) by a vetted judge. Evidence would be kept secret from the defendants so as to protect the sources of MI5, MI6 and the

Government Communications Headquarters (GCHQ), those from a third state like the United States – this would also entail 'special advocates', state-vetted defence lawyers who could be trusted not to pass on intelligence information.

As the evidence presented would come from intelligence and security sources Blunkett said that:

> 'It needs to be presented in a way that does not allow disclosure by any of the parties involved, which would destroy your security services. It is about the threshold of evidence and the nature of those involved being accredited and trusted not to reveal sources.'

The government wanted to look at the 'evidential base and the threshold of evidence'. The level of proof, Blunkett argued, could be lowered from 'beyond reasonable doubt' to the 'balance of probabilities'. He said he intended to publish his proposals in an options paper on anti-terrorist laws.

The reaction to the proposals was immediate. Baroness Helena Kennedy QC said they were 'an affront to the rule of law' and that 'he really is a shameless authoritarian'. Louise Christian, a lawyer representing a number of those held in Guantanamo Bay, said: 'I don't think he is fit to be Home Secretary'. Newspaper editorials weighed in against Blunkett's proposals; a *Guardian* editorial said that by refusing to 'seek a balance between public safety and the rule of law, he loses all sympathy'.

On 7 February 2004, six of the leading lawyers in the country, Nick Blake QC, Andrew Nicol QC, Manjit Singh QC, Ian Macdonald QC, Rick Scannell and Tom de la Mare wrote an 'open letter' condemning the proposals which:

> 'would contradict three cardinal principles of criminal justice: a public trial by an impartial judge and jury of one's peers, proof of guilt beyond reasonable doubt, and a right to know, comment on and respond to the case being made against the accused.'

David Blunkett's 'kite-flying' seemed, at the time, just that; however, it transpires that it reflected ongoing, secret discussions in the G8 (see below).

On 18 December 2003, the Privy Counsellors Review Committee published a critical report on the Anti-Terrorism, Crime and Security Act 2001 (ATCSA 2001, Part IV[2]), but the government did not respond to it.[3] The Home Secretary's proposal for pre-emptive action was not mentioned in the Home Office options paper published at the end of February 2004.[4] It did say that the internment of foreign nationals was 'essential', but that the extension of these powers to British citizens would be a big step:

> 'such draconian powers would be difficult to justify.'

The options paper did float the idea of introducing 'civil orders' against people suspected of fund-raising or propaganda work on the 'periphery' of terrorist organisations.[5]

Of direct relevance to the use of security and intelligence evidence in court – where it is provided by a third state – is a judgment given in the Court of Appeal on 11 August 2004. Considering an appeal by ten men held under the Anti-

Terrorism, Crime and Security Act 2001, the judges, by two to one, declared that the state could use evidence in court from other countries without having to investigate whether it was gathered as a result of torture or ill-treatment. The only proviso was that United Kingdom agencies should not be involved. Lord Justice Laws, one of the two in the majority, said he could not believe:

> 'he [the Home Secretary] may be presented with information of great potential importance, where there is, let us say, a suspicion as to the means by which, in another jurisdiction, it has been obtained. What is he to do?'

How could the law:

> 'sensibly impose on the Secretary of State a duty of solemn inquiry as to the interrogation methods used by agencies of other sovereign states. Apart from the practical unreality, I can find no sound juridical base for the imposition of such a requirement.'

The court of appeal had backed the government position. In the House of Lords Home Office Minister, Baroness Scotland, had told Lord Judd that:

> 'Save for evidence that is obtained from a party (usually the defendant in a criminal trial) all evidence is admissible, however unlawfully obtained.'

This view does not seem to square with the United Kingdom's ratification of the UN Convention Against Torture (Article 15) which says that:

> 'any statement which is established to have been made as a result of torture shall not be invoked as evidence in any proceedings'

Unless this judgment is overturned when it comes up on appeal in the House of Lords it will leave the door wide open to the introduction – without any questions being asked – of evidence in court gathered by torture or inhuman treatment (as long as the United Kingdom is not involved in the torture). No questions could be asked regardless of the state from which it came or the proven history of the use of such technique by the agencies of that state.

The Commissioner for Human Rights for the Council of Europe, Alvaro Gil-Robles, added his voice of opposition to internment without trial under the Anti-Terrorism, Crime and Security Act 2001 and the United Kingdom's derogation from the European Convention on Human Rights. He said he did not believe an emergency existed which could justify such powers, and that he was also concerned about police powers to detain people for up to 14 days without charge, and the disproportionate use of stop and search against Muslims. He was to issue a report on the United Kingdom in January 2005.

The judgment by the law lords (the highest court in the United Kingdom) on 16 December 2004, that detention without charge or trial is unlawful, was decided by eight to one.[6] Lord Hoffman said that what was called into question is:

> 'the very existence of an ancient liberty of which this country has until now been very proud: freedom from arbitrary arrest and detention'.

Even more damning was his conclusion that:

> 'The real threat to the life of the nation ... comes not from terrorism but from laws such as these'.

The overall view of the judges was expressed by Lady Hale who said:

> 'Executive detention is the antithesis of the right to liberty and security of the person. Yet this is what the 2001 Act allows. We have always taken it for granted that we cannot be locked up in this country without trial or explanation'.

'Control orders'

On 26 January 2005, the new Home Secretary, Charles Clarke, announced in response to the law lords judgment that the government intended to replace Part 4 of the Anti-Terrorism, Crime and Security Act 2001.[7] He said that the government had considered the use of intercept material as evidence in court but some was inadmissible and some, if used, could compromise national security and its methods, damage 'relationships with foreign powers or intelligence agencies', or put 'the lives of sources at risk'.[8] He also said that the government was seeking to deport some of those held in Belmarsh prison providing 'assurances' as to their treatment could be obtained – the detained men are from Algeria, Tunisia, Egypt and Jordan[9].

Part 4 powers under the Anti-Terrorism, Crime and Security Act 2001 were replaced by the Prevention of Terrorism Act 2005 with a new system of 'control orders' covering British citizens and foreigners alike and external and internal threat of terrorism (thus covering Northern Ireland, too).[10] The Prevention of Terrorism Bill was finally passed on 11 March 2005.[11]

It took just 13 working days for parliament to pass the Act because of a government imposed timetable 'guillotine'. The final government 'compromise' is a bit complicated and is not in the Act itself. The government, in the form of the Home Secretary, said that they intended to present a new Counter-Terrorism Bill to set out 'preparatory' offences for terrorist-related activities in the autumn. It would be discussed in parliament at the same time as the first annual review of the Prevention of Terrorism Act 2005. Moreover, MPs and peers would be given parliamentary time to seek to amend the Prevention of Terrorism Act 2005. The 'compromise' is based on a 'promise'.

Article 1.3 of the Act sets out the powers 'to make control orders'. The 'Secretary of State' (ie: the Home Secretary) is empowered to make an order against an individual and set out the conditions (eg: tagging) for suspected 'terrorist related activity'. The range of 'control orders' is set out in Clause 1.4 and includes:
– prohibition of having 'specified articles' in their possession (eg: a mobile phone)
– prohibition of having access to 'specified services' (eg: the internet)
– restriction on work or occupation
– restriction of 'association' with 'specified persons' or 'other persons generally'
– restriction on place of residence and who can visit
– restriction on movement to an area or region
– restriction on movement *'to, from or within the United Kingdom'* (including

surrendering passport)
- to give access at all times of 'specified persons' (police and Special Branch) to residence
- to allow searches at any times of the residence[12] plus being required to wear a 'tag' and – 'house arrest' (Clause 1.5)

Charles Clarke, the Home Secretary, has admitted that control orders could result in a similar scenario with the family and friends of the individual being subject to the same constraints.[13]

Control orders (of both kinds) can be imposed for 12 months and can be renewed on 'one or more occasions'. There is nothing to stop control orders from becoming virtually permanent. If a person breaks the conditions of an order they can be sent to prison for up to five years without there being any further judicial examination of the case against them – they can be sent to prison without a trial taking place.

These sixteen conditions are termed 'non-derogating', though Ben Emmerson QC argues that a combination of control orders would constitute a breach of the Convention.[14] A 'derogating control order' (from the European Convention on Human Rights) is where a person is placed under 'house arrest' (1.5). The issuing of 'non-derogating' control orders is simply based on 'reasonable grounds for suspecting' a person is involved in terrorist-related activities. The judiciary then has to confirm the order, but within very restricted conditions which are a far cry from a judge-made decision. The government is only obliged to show the judge sufficient 'intelligence' to convince them of the need for a control order (not the whole intelligence dossier). The role of the judges is defined as being governed by the rules of a 'judicial review', which is not at all the same as a full hearing of all the evidence and then the judge making the decision.

In effect the judiciary will be asked to confirm the decision of the minister and can only overturn both the decision and the conditions imposed if they are: 'obviously flawed'. In other words, the judiciary can only reject the minister's decision if there is absolute evidence that it is wrong. It is no wonder that the judiciary are concerned that they will be caught up in a process for which they will take part of the blame.

At the initial hearing – when a non-derogating or derogating order has been issued by the minister – the court can hear the application without the suspect being present (3.5.a), without the suspect even having been notified (3.5.b), and without the accused being given the opportunity of making any representation to the court (3.5.c).

For derogating control orders the initial hearing – on a application by the minister – only has to agree that there are 'reasonable grounds for believing' it is necessary. Also at this initial hearing the hands of the judges are also tied because a control order can be issued where:

> 'there is material which (if not disproved) is capable of being relied on by the court as establishing that the individual is or has been involved in terrorism-related activity (4.3.a).'

It is very hard to see how the 'material' could be 'disproved' as the person will not be present, will not know the evidence against them, and will not be represented. It is only at the first full hearing that the judgment will be based on the 'balance of probabilities'.

The Schedule to the Act sets out the details of the court proceedings. A judge must ensure that:

> 'disclosures of information are not made where they would be contrary to the national interest' (Section 11.2).

The 'rules of court' will be drawn up by the Lord Chancellor (Section 11.3). These 'rules of court' include 'the mode of proof', enabling or requiring proceedings to be determined without a hearing (Section 11.4.1).

Most crucially the 'rules of court' can makes provisions for control order proceedings or appeals:

> 'to take place without the full particulars of the reasons for the decisions to which the proceedings relate being given to a relevant party to the proceedings or his legal representative' (Section 11.4.2a).

The proceedings can also take place in 'the absence' of the person concerned and their lawyer (Section 11.4.2b). The person will only receive a 'summary of evidence taken in his absence' (Section 11.4.2.d). This 'summary' is to be prepared by the Home Secretary. The Home Secretary is to give the hearings all 'relevant material' – which, of course, may only be that necessary to convince rather than the full 'intelligence assessment' provided by MI5, on which the initial decision was taken.

The 'interests' of the 'suspect' are to be 'represented' by special advocates, appointed by the Attorney-General, who will not be allowed to communicate with the 'suspect' or their lawyers (Section 11.7).

'Terrorist-related' activity is defined in Article 1.9 as the 'commission, preparation or instigation of acts of terrorism' (which it might be thought would already be criminal offences) or 'conduct which gives support or assistance to individuals who are known or believed to be involved in terrorist-related activity' or:

> 'conduct which gives **encouragement** to the commission, preparation or instigation of such acts, or which is intended to do so' (emphasis added).

The term 'encouragement' is not defined. The scope of the term 'encouragement' is compounded by the overall provision for Clause 1.9 which says it is:

> 'immaterial whether the acts of terrorism in question are specific acts of terrorism of acts of terrorism in general.'

The proposed offence of 'encouragement' for 'acts of terrorism generally' is suspiciously close to the highly contentious concept of *'apologie'* being proposed in the Council of Europe draft Convention on Terrorism which could endanger free speech and freedom of the press (see below).

Under the Prevention of Terrorism Act 2005, all meaningful proceedings will take place *in camera* (press and public excluded), without the defendant present – who will thus not know the evidence against him, nor will his lawyer.

The differences between judicial scrutiny and normal criminal procedure are important. If an individual is formally charged with terrorist offences the trial would be before a judge and jury and the defendant would know the evidence against him. Some evidence may be presented in camera with the public excluded and witnesses may appear by video link or give evidence from behind a screen to protect their identity. On the other hand, 'independent judicial scrutiny' means a hearing before a judge(s) but no jury. The defendant and his lawyers will not hear or see the evidence. The only people to hear the evidence will be the judge and the 'special advocates' appointed by the Attorney-General to try and put forward the views of the defendant, and they are not allowed to tell the defendant what the evidence is against him or ask him for his views to contradict the 'evidence'.

One of the arguments advanced by Charles Clarke, the Home Secretary, and by John Denham, ex-Home Minister and chair of the Home Affairs Select Committee, is that other countries in the European Union can hold people suspected of terrorist activities for up to four years. This is a disingenuous argument. It is true that countries such as Spain and Germany, for example, can hold people in 'preventive detention', usually for up to two years in Germany and three years in Spain. In Spain people may be held where: 1) there is a danger that the person may flee, 2) or that they may destroy evidence, or 3) that they may repeat the alleged offence. The same goes for Germany where people can also be held for suspected participation in a terrorist organisation. But, and this is the crucial difference, in both countries:

a) 'preventive detention' can only be ordered by a judge
b) the defendant can appoint a lawyer of their choice
c) the state has to present sufficient evidence in court to justify detention – the defendant knows the evidence against them
d) the defence can question the evidence and the grounds for detention (eg: fleeing).

This is a judicial process, in a court with evidence presented to the defendant which can be questioned, and the defendant has full rights – not a decision by a government minister.

As the first control orders were issued it emerged that private security firms were to be responsible for carrying out some of the surveillance of the individuals. The Home Office's 'Regulatory Assessment' of the costs of the Act says:

> 'There will be costs to the police/Home Office in terms of monitoring the Orders but where possible these will be contracted out to private companies as per existing arrangements. Systems are already in place for monitoring criminals released on licence and other offenders'[15]

And the experience of those placed under control orders imposes an almost life on them and their families.[16]

The use of 'intelligence information'

'Control orders' are to be based, Charles Clarke told parliament:

> 'on the basis of an intelligence assessment provided by the Security Service [where] there are reasonable grounds for suspecting that an individual is, or has been, concerned with terrorism'

which means that *all sources of intelligence* can be included – whether from the United Kingdom or external sources (such as the United States).

When the Home Secretary made a statement on 26 January 2005, a number of MPs asked why intercept evidence (that is, from telephone-tapping) could not be used in court? This could ensure that a person could be formally charged and brought before a criminal court. A number of newspaper editorials and individuals pursued the same line of argument. It is also being 'pedalled' in the media that 'intercept evidence' is allowed in other European countries so why not here, too? Javier Solana, the High Representative of the Council of the European Union, said the same during an ITV television interview by Jonathan Dimbleby, and said that not to use intercept material was 'naive' (6.2.05).[17]

However, when the United Kingdom Home Secretary talks about getting an 'intelligence assessment' from MI5 (Security Service), he is *not* talking just about phone 'intercept' evidence.[18] The Home Secretary is talking about a range of 'intelligence evidence' on which he would base a decision to issue a control order from a variety of sources including:

– telephone conversations from fixed phones and mobile phones (including the locations of both parties), plus text messages
– faxes
– e-mails (including the location of both parties) with both traffic data and full contents of the communications
– 'bugging' (covert listening device) and video evidence
– internet usage (web sites visited and pages/files downloaded)
– from tracking devices on vehicles and/or people and/or an object containing a tracking device
– surveillance photos and video
– reports and statements from covert sources (informers or undercover agents) of varying degrees of reliability and accuracy (judged on a scale of 1-5).
– open source material (such as press cuttings)
– employment, bank, credit card, health records, vehicle and insurance details
– travel details, especially to and from 'dubious' states and/or regarding suspect individuals/groups
– membership or association with 'suspect' organisations
– in addition all of the above from a European Union agency (eg: Europol and/or SitCen) or member state agencies
– in addition all of the above from non-European Union state agencies (eg: the United States), which may include statements gathered through the use of torture and ill-treatment, and sources/witnesses would not be available for cross-

examination.

It is for this reason that the government wants to retain the power to issue an executive order (control order) rather than cede this initial decision to a court. Equally they are assuming that in the closed hearings of a judicial review only a fraction of the underlying intelligence would have to be revealed – just sufficient 'evidence' to convince. This view is confirmed in the Bill (Schedule 4.3.c) which states that the Secretary of State does not have to disclose 'anything' which will not be relied on in court.

The introduction of intelligence as 'evidence' presents major problems and consequences. Would, for example, evidence of an intercepted phone conversation include all the conversations or just the one singled out by the security agencies? Would the full text of the intercept be available to the court and the defence or just selections from it? Would a statement from an unnamed source, probably called person 'A', (ie: an informer or infiltrated agent or a person being held in custody) be acceptable? Would the defence be allowed to question the source? How could the defence question a statement if the origin was from outside the United Kingdom, for example, from the United States, Saudi Arabian or Egyptian agencies? The question of evidence gathered through the use of torture has yet to be considered by the law lords.[19]

Four British men held in Gauntanamo Bay for over three years were released in January 2005. On their return to the UK they were questioned by anti-terrorist police, then released without charge a day later. However, the men have now been told by the Home Secretary that they pose a terrorist threat to the United Kingdom, and that they are banned from travelling abroad, and are to be denied passports.[20] In a letter to them the Home Secretary states:

> 'On the basis of the information which has come to light during your detention by the United States, the Home Secretary considered that there are strong grounds for believing that, on leaving the United Kingdom, you would take part in activities against the United Kingdom or allied targets.'

The men and their lawyers say that any admissions made while being held in Guantanamo Bay are false and were made under duress (ranging from torture to ill-treatment). On the basis of 'intelligence' supplied by the United States the men have been denied the freedom of movement.

'Control orders' could be used by the security agencies (MI5 and the Special Branch) to target 'activist' or suspected 'ringleaders' and result in dozens of Muslims being criminalised. Already the agencies use the Terrorism Act 2000, the Anti-Terrorism, Crime and Security Act 2001, and stop and search powers to 'disrupt' suspected groups against whom they have no evidence of a terrorist offence.[21]

At present the United Kingdom is the only country in the European Union which has chosen to take exceptional measures. But behind the scenes a new agenda is being set by the G8 which will affect the whole of the European Union.

How the G8 is setting the agenda

The United Kingdom Home Secretary's proposals, back in February 2004, did not happen simply by chance. The origin of these proposals came from a much higher source – the G8, where Home Office, MI5 and MI6 officials are key players (alongside the United States).[22]

The role of the G8 took on a new dimension after 11 September 2001. It is a 'global' grouping which can set global standards. Two of its first demands were for international standards for biometrics on passports, and the retention of telecommunications traffic data – the first of which has been agreed by the European Union and the second is now going through its legislative process – neither, as yet, has even been proposed in the United States. Another was for checking and surveillance of all visitors entering a country – the United States has introduced this, and the European Union is about to (commonly known as checking 'PNR', Passenger Name Records, against 'watch-lists').[23] It is also of relevance to note four G8 members already intern/detain people without charge and trial – the United States, United Kingdom, Russia and Canada.[24]

As the ideology of the 'war on terrorism' deepened and became permanent, other standards were set out by the G8. Notable in this context are the G8 recommendations on transnational crime which were 'endorsed' by the G8 Ministers of Justice and Interior Ministers at Mont-Tremblant in Canada on 13-14 May 2002.[25] Although referring to 'transnational crime', the recommendations were directed at 'transnational crime and terrorism'.[26]

Among the key recommendations is a section on 'strengthening investigative capabilities', including 'Investigative techniques'. Even among the G8 countries, let alone the European Union and the rest of the world, the use of telephone-tapping, bugging and video surveillance, informers, *agent-provocateurs,* and undercover agents is stringently circumscribed in law – in many European Union countries judicial authorisation is required to carry out covert surveillance.[27]

For example, in seven European Union states the police require judicial authorisation to access 'documentation of telephone tapping' and in a further nine states they cannot obtain this information without judicial authorisation. For 'documentation of room bugging' eight states require judicial authorisation to access it and in a further nine states they cannot obtain this information without judicial authorisation. In nine states 'real-time' telecom monitoring requires judicial authorisation to access and in fourteen states they do this without judicial authorisation. As to access to traffic data held by service providers, in nine states the police require judicial authorisation, and thirteen states cannot obtain this information without judicial authorisation. 'Judicial authorisation' is seen within the G8 plans as an 'obstacle' to efficient cooperation between agencies – both internally and externally.

The use of such investigative techniques is perceived as being exceptional and their everyday use associated with authoritarian states. In May 2002 this G8 meeting agreed on:

'the relevance and effectiveness of special investigative techniques such as electronic or other forms of surveillance technology, undercover operations and controlled deliveries.'[28]

G8 states were called on to review their:

'domestic arrangements for those techniques, also ensuring any necessary anonymity of undercover agents and to conclude, where necessary, appropriate bilateral and multilateral agreements and arrangements for using the special investigative techniques in the context of cooperation at international level...'

This commitment is immediately followed by the following recommendation:

'We emphasise the importance of giving the fullest possible protection to sensitive information received from other states. The competent authorities of different states should advise each other as to the requirements regarding the disclosure of information in the course of judicial and administrative proceedings, and discuss in advance potential difficulties arising from those requirements.'

From this point on there is an ongoing link between 'special investigative techniques' and how to allow the product of surveillance to be used – whether by other 'friendly' agencies or in 'judicial proceedings'.[29]

The meeting of G8 Ministers of Justice and Home Affairs in Paris on 5 May 2003 (prior to the Evian G8 Summit) reiterated the need to 'promote special investigative techniques' and called on their 'experts' to 'identify the obstacles' to international judicial cooperation in this area.

United States takes over the Presidency of G8

The United States took over the Presidency of G8 on 1 January 2004 and sent out a questionnaire to its member states drawn up by the 'Roma Group'.

On 23 February 2004, there was a European Union-United States high-level officials meeting on justice and home affairs under the 'New Transatlantic Agenda', held in Dublin. The Irish Presidency Chair of the European Union's Article 36 Committee, assisted by officials, met with their US counterparts. The meeting was an: 'EU-US Troika JHA Informal/SCIFA Informal Troika' (Troika refers to past, present and next EU presidency).[30] The report on the meeting is peppered with references to on-going work in G8 (of which neither Ireland nor the next EU Presidency, Netherlands, are members).[31]

At the meeting, the United States took the lead on the topic of 'Terrorism prevention measures' and 'expressed three concerns regarding [EU Member] States abilities to fight terrorism':

'The first concern was that states' legal systems should allow their law enforcement authorities to take action against preparatory acts for terrorism at a stage where no terrorist acts had been committed.'

The second US concern was the ability of European Union states to:

'afford mutual legal assistance and extradite persons for preparatory acts.'

While the third:

> 'probably most difficult issue which was raised by the US was how to share intelligence information related to terrorism for use in a criminal proceeding in another country, while ensuring that the intelligence would be protected.
>
> This question is two-pronged: (1) have states the legal ability to protect intelligence information, and (2) how can the (prosecutorial) authorities of a state be informed of the fact that another state holds intelligence information which is relevant to the terrorist case that is being prosecuted. The US clearly signalled that it was seeking to cooperate with the EU and its Member States on this issue. As a first step it suggested drawing up a document that would collate information from the US and the Member States, which would lay out to what extent and how states can protect intelligence information received from another country.
>
> The G8 had already started work on this by way of a questionnaire that had been sent out to and replied by all G8 members. The US suggested that the EU might consider following up on this questionnaire in relation to use of intelligence information.'

In summation the United States said that:
1. law enforcement agencies should be 'allowed' to take action against preparatory acts for terrorism where no such act has been committed.
2. extradition should be allowed for 'preparatory acts'.
3. intelligence 'information' should be used in court while ensuring it is 'protected'.

Even as the United States was canvassing the European Union to support these ideas, it was preparing to put a series of issues openly and explicitly on the table at the G8 meeting of Justice and Home Affairs Ministers in Washington on 11 May 2004 – it should be remembered that of the now 25 European Union member states only the United Kingdom, France, Italy and Germany have a say (the European Commission is also in attendance).

The press release from the Washington meeting again linked the use of 'advanced investigative techniques' with the 'sharing' of intelligence to:

> 'better prevent and disrupt terrorist activities and to prosecute terrorists.'

There were three detailed recommendations on:
- 'special investigative techniques' [32];
- 'enhancing the legal framework to prevent terrorist attacks'[33];
- protecting intelligence in prosecutions.[34]

The Lyon and Roma groups, under the French and United States G8 Presidencies, had conducted a survey of 'special investigative techniques' which led to the recommendation that 'legal systems' should 'allow' the use of techniques such as:

> 'use of undercover agents, use of covert filing and listening devices, and covert interception of all forms of electronic communications.'

Seven recommendations follow including:
a. the use of 'special investigative techniques to support *criminal proceedings* at national and international levels' (emphasis added)
b. the creation of a 'legal framework' which allows the use of 'special investigative techniques'
c. 'access to a broad array of special investigative techniques for the purpose of international investigation'
d. here the recommendation (no 6) makes a direct link between the use of the 'techniques' and the use of their product in court:

> 'Requested States should work with requesting States to maximise the likelihood of admissibility in the requesting State of evidence provided through special investigative techniques.

The mere fact that a special investigative technique, carried out by the requested State in accordance with its law, would not be available to the requesting State in similar circumstances, *should not per se bar the use of evidence so acquired in the requesting State's courts*' (emphasis added).

This could mean, for example, that the United States could request a European Union state to conduct blanket electronic surveillance of a particular group based in the European Union and this 'intelligence' could be used in the United States where this power may not exist (or, at least, not the power to produce such intelligence 'intercepts' by US agencies in its courts). Similarly, it covers tapes or statements from people held in states where the use of torture or inhuman treatment in suspected terrorist cases is the norm.

The second recommendation covers creating a 'legal framework to prevent terrorist attacks'. The emphasis here is on people and groups suspected of preparatory acts requiring action in:

> 'situations in which the terrorist objective is not yet well defined and an attack may not happen for some time... prevention, investigation and prosecution are complimentary in nature...'

The objective is to take action against people and groups 'prior to terrorist attacks being carried out'. What this means is not spelt out. Does this refer to people who are buying, gathering and collecting materials which could be used in an attack? If so, this would be understandable. Does it mean people with 'radical' views, who may have visited Pakistan or Afghanistan in the past and who consort with others, some of whom have done the same? If so, this would be unacceptable.

The recommendation calls for criminal offences covering 'recruiting persons to commit terrorist acts' (which is clear) and providing 'directly or indirectly' financial or other 'material support' and:

> 'a person who engages in such conduct should be criminally liable not only where he or she knows or intends that the conduct will facilitate the commission of a specific attack, but also where he or she knows or intends that the conduct will facilitate the commission of future unspecified attacks.'

The latter category is not clear. Does the giving of a mobile phone to someone constitute such conduct? The person may have 'radical views' but in giving the phone how is intention to be judged? Does the giving of a pair of boots, which end up in Chechnya in the hands of a suspected Al Qaeda group, constitute giving 'material support'?[35]

Another recommendation specifically refers to social, religious and charitable groups who should also be subject to 'special investigative techniques':

> 'while duly respecting established legal privileges recognised under domestic law, such as attorney-client or clergyman-penitent confidentiality and respect for diplomatic status, the fact of involvement of entities whether social, religious or charitable in nature, or of their leaders should not per se bar use of investigative techniques.'

This set of recommendations calls for i) the use of bribes ('incentives') to gather intelligence; ii) those defined above as 'directly or indirectly' suspected of giving material support to be extraditable for 'anticipatory or preparatory' offences; iii) states should 'assist another country' by conducting 'a broad array of special investigative techniques' against targets at their request.

The third set of recommendations covers the use of 'intelligence' gathered through 'special investigative techniques' in the 'prosecution of terrorists and their associates' while giving:

> 'appropriate protection to national security intelligence information in criminal prosecutions.'

The recommendations call on states to:
1. 'adopt legislation' and 'procedural safeguards' to 'prevent, disrupt and pre-empt' terrorist activities by permitting:

> 'information sharing among and between their intelligence community, their law enforcement community and their prosecutors, to the fullest possible degree.'

2. 'adopt legislation' to establish 'procedural safeguards' which will:

> 'permit national security intelligence information to be used in the prosecution of terrorists and those who commit associated offences, while protecting such information, including sources and methods by which such information has been acquired; *to the extent possible* consistent with a fair trial, such mechanisms, for example, include the use of summaries, substitutions or stipulations' (emphasis added).

What is meant by 'summaries'? It implies that the agencies will be able to present an edited version of an intercept or statement from an informer? Does 'substitution' mean getting rid of juries and introducing judge-only 'Diplock' courts? And does 'stipulations' mean that defence lawyers will have to be vetted and defendants not allowed to see the 'evidence' against them?

3. 'adopt legislation' allowing: 'national security intelligence information' from a third state to be 'used in a criminal proceeding' subject to:

> 'the conditions, if any, agreed upon between the competent authorities in the originating State and those in the receiving State'

If 'legislation' to this effect were adopted the 'conditions' agreed between intelligence agencies would override the power of the courts to decide otherwise.

4. in 'adopting' this 'legislation' states should:

> 'give due regard to civil liberties and fundamental principles of law.'

Well, enough said.

Taken together these recommendations would totally undermine any concept of a fair trial and the presumption of innocence. They would 'legalise' the pre-emptive detention of those held in Belmarsh who are being held on unseen 'evidence' provided by United Kingdom intelligence and security agencies.[36]

The G8 Sea Island Summit in the United States on 8-10 June 2004 simply noted the recommendations from the Justice and Home Affairs Ministers in Washington on 11 May 2004.

The United States handed over Presidency of the G8 to the United Kingdom on 1 January 2005.

The European Union-United States Summit at Dromoland Castle, Ireland on 26 June 2004

It might be thought that the 25 member states in the European Union could act independently of its four G8 members – the United Kingdom, Germany, France and Italy. After all, only the United Kingdom had attempted to 'pre-empt' alleged terrorist activity by imprisoning seventeen men under its Anti-Terrorism, Crime and Security Act 2001 without trial – and is the only European Union member state to derogate from Article 5 of the European Convention on Human Rights.

However, at the European Union-United States Summit in Ireland on 26 June 2004 the 'European Union-United States Declaration on combating terrorism' agreed to 'take forward... objectives, through dialogue and action at all levels' including twelve 'objectives' to 'detect, investigate and prosecute terrorists and prevent terrorist attacks'.[37] The wording in the Declaration will seem familiar by now and includes:

> '3.3 We will work together to enhance, in accordance with national legislation, our abilities to share information among intelligence and law enforcement agencies to prevent and disrupt terrorist activities, and to better use sensitive information as allowed by national legislation in aid of prosecutions of terrorists in a manner which protects the information, while ensuring a fair trial' [European Union doc no: 10809/04]

There should be:

– 'appropriate legislation in place to investigate and prosecute *offences linked to terrorist activities*' (3.4)

- A new criminal offence of 'knowingly supplying or attempting to supply material or logistic support' should be created (3.5).
- The use of 'investigative techniques' should be promoted (3.6)
- and 'proposals directed at improving the exchange of personal information for the purposes of combating terrorism' will be regularly reviewed (3.7).
- Cooperation between 'US prosecutors and Eurojust' should be strengthened (3.9)
- the European Union-United States agreements on extradition and mutual legal assistance should be 'rapidly' completed so that joint investigation teams and 'enhanced cooperation' (eg: including requests for surveillance and intercepts from the USA) can be effected (3.10).

And, finally, there should be improved:

> 'co-operation on the sharing of law enforcement and other sensitive information between government agencies consistent with national legislation, and the need to protect sources and fair procedures' (3.12).

The swift endorsement by the European Union of the central demands of the G8 and the United States comes as no surprise to observers who have watched the extensive build-up of European Union-United States cooperation and high-level meetings on justice and home affairs since the beginning of 2002 – evidence of the emerging United States-European Union 'axis' on the 'war on terrorism' (as distinct from their differences on the war against the 'axis of evil').

The Dromoland Declaration was followed up at the 'European Union-United States Justice and Home Affairs Informal High Level' meeting at Wassenaar, Netherlands on 7 July 2004. The United States side 'emphasised that not every item in the Declaration could be finalised' quickly and that 'it was advisable to prioritise' – there were 42 points in the Declaration. The third 'priority' point was 'Preparatory (anticipatory crime)':

> 'The US raised the issue of joint EU-US forces aiming at a systematic approach to prevent terrorist acts. The US was interested in adopting and implementing a prevention strategy, defining minimum level provisions on crimes in preparation, legal competence on mutual legal assistance and extradition and a more difficult issue, the sharing of information subject to data protection.'

The minutes of the meeting state: 'The questionnaire on the use of intelligence in criminal court cases was discussed' and 'The [Netherlands] Presidency concluded that the European Union and the United States would cooperate as agreed in the EU-US Declaration.'

The European Union initiative is launched

Just three weeks after the High Level European Union-United States meeting in Wassenaar, on 28 July 2004, the Netherlands Presidency of the Council sent a questionnaire to the Working Party on Substantive Criminal Law for member states to respond to by 1 September 2004.[38]

The reason for the circulation of the 'Questionnaire on prevention of terrorism' was because:

> 'the US authorities have conveyed several concerns regarding States' abilities to fight terrorism.
>
> A first concern relates to the ability of law enforcement authorities to take action against preparatory acts for terrorism at a stage where no terrorist acts had been committed. A second concern related to the ability of states to afford mutual legal assistance and extradite persons for preparatory acts. The third issue which has been raised by the US is how to share intelligence information related to terrorism for use in criminal proceedings in another country, while ensuring that the intelligence is protected.'

It should come as no surprise that the questionnaire sent out to the 25 European Union member states was the same questionnaire already answered by all G8 members. The questionnaire is primarily directed at the first and third of the United States' 'concerns' – the introduction of a preparatory criminal offence and the protection of intelligence information in court proceedings. It opens by asking if it is a crime in their countries to 'incite or recruit' for terrorist acts (A.1) and to provide 'directly or indirectly' material support (A.2).

The next question (A.3) makes explicit the distinction between current criminal offences directed at acts committed or knowingly of the planned commission of a terrorist act and the new concept of 'preparatory' or 'associated' offences. The questionnaire asks:

> 'Can liability also arise where there is a more general mental state, such as where the recruiter/inciter/supporter intends to, or knows that his or her conduct will aid future unspecified terrorist acts?'

It is also asked whether there are legal limits on action against religious leaders or charitable institutions (A.4) and whether financial inducements before an attack or after are lawful?

The second series of questions opens with the use of 'special investigative techniques' (B.1), including:

> 'can the government overtly or covertly observe conduct taking place in a house of worship or property otherwise belonging to a religious or charitable entity? Can electronic surveillance be conducted in such a location? Are there limitations to executing searches and seizures in such a location?'

It goes on to ask whether a 'religious figure' can be lawfully questioned or information gathered about them, and do any 'legal privileges' bar gathering such information of evidence? (B.2) And are there any legal limits on detaining or arresting religious figures? (B.3)

The question on the use of 'intelligence' in court (B.4) follows:

> 'To what extent do you have procedures under your law that permit the use in judicial proceedings of national security intelligence information in a manner that protects its source while adequately protecting rights of the defence?'

The final question asks whether a European Union state can assist a non-European Union state (for example, the United States) in:

> 'gathering information and evidence by other countries for use in their criminal investigations or prosecutions?'

It then explicitly uses as an example the surveillance and bugging of a place of worship.

The term 'mutual legal assistance' is a euphemism for acts such as this. For example, can the United States request that a European Union member state either place a targeted person(s) under surveillance and give the intelligence 'product' to them or, as the above phraseology suggests, allowing (and aiding) US agencies to carry out the surveillance of the 'target(s)?'[39]

– The response to the European Union questionnaire

As far as can be ascertained only 11 out of 25 European Union member states have responded to the questionnaire. Some member states responded by setting out the current legal situation in their countries with little further comment (for example, Germany and Portugal).[40] A number of member states said that the Framework Decision on combating terrorism (13.6.02) already covered terrorist acts including preparatory and accessory acts.

Slovakia said:

> 'Its practical use would be improved if the American party could be confronted with the same questions too.'

The Czech Republic said the same.

Belgium, Ireland and Austria thought it would be 'very useful' if the European Union G8 members were to inform the rest of the European Union of their responses. It also proposed that any questionnaire should be drafted by all the parties so that each could make amendments and that information should be shared between all the partners – including the United States.

Greece was not convinced that these 'American style' measures were needed and wanted to know how intelligence information could be protected. It was concerned, too, over lack of mention of the European Convention on Human Rights, reciprocity, the death penalty, and data protection.

Austria expressed strong concerns about a 'shift' in what is perceived as criminal which could put the rights of suspects at risk and infringe freedom of religious expression. For example, the line between the procurement of intelligence information and its use in prosecutions not revealing sources.

Germany was the only European Union member of the G8 to supply the same answers to the questionnaire as it gave to the G8 – a basic statement of the current legal position in Germany.

The United Kingdom's response – which did not include its response to the G8 questionnaire – is very revealing. The United Kingdom's view is that the questions are 'pertinent to the concerns of the United States' and that:

> 'the burden of completing such questionnaires can be considerable, and we wonder whether this is the most cost-effective means of addressing this issue.

It might be preferable for the G8 to put forward a set of preliminary proposals and invite European Union Member States to comment on them, including the extent to which they are already compliant and any legal or other impediments they foresee to their becoming compliant.'

In other words, the United Kingdom's view is that the G8 should be in charge of initiating these proposals and that European Union member states should set out any problems with becoming *'compliant'* to its demands. There could not be a clearer expression of how the United Kingdom views the European Union and how the 'Atlantic Alliance' of the United Kingdom and the United States reflects their dominant role within G8.

The Council's Working Party on Substantive Criminal Law discussed the issue at its meeting on 8-9 September 2004 and a 'number of delegations' asked for clarification as to the aim of the questionnaire. 'Certain delegations' also asked for the distribution of the responses of European Union members of the G8 to its questionnaire. The matter was referred upwards to the Article 36 Committee.

The high-level Article 36 Committee discussed the issue at its meeting on 7-8 October 2004 and concluded that the Presidency should contact the United States to see how it 'would like to proceed' and ask for a copy of the US reply to the G8 questionnaire (European Union states in G8 should also make their responses available). This response might seem to indicate a luke-warm response to the United States (and United Kingdom) demand. However, the influence of top Justice and Home Affairs officials in the Council (and Commission) who meet and discuss with their United States counterparts regularly, and who take part in G8 working groups, should not be under-estimated.

Council of the European Union takes up the initiative

The proposal for using intelligence information as evidence in court was raised within the closed circles of the Council of the European Union in an unreleased review of its work to combat terrorism early in 2004. This report from the Council's General Secretariat to COREPER (the committee of permanent representatives of the member states based in Brussels) said:

'One of the main problems to be addressed is the use of intelligence as evidence in courts in full respect of the right of defence.'

In an 'evaluation report' by Mr Vries, the European Union Counter-Terrorism Coordinator (based in the Council), produced at the end of May 2004, asks:

'How can intelligence be exploited so that it can be used, if necessary, by courts in legal proceedings?' [EU doc no: 9876/04] [41]

A 'more integrated approach' is 'desirable' to the sharing of information between different state databases (for example, police and customs) and it should be considered whether:

'security services could also have a permanent access to law enforcement databases and to other relevant administrative databases, such as border management ones.'

The report also noted that some internal security services had legal powers for the 'interception of communications or eavesdropping' while:

> 'In some Member States, there is no specific legal framework relating to special investigative techniques.'

The updated 'EU Plan of Action on Combating Terrorism' agreed at the European Union Summit (meeting of prime ministers) in December 2004 reflected developments on some of the issues raised in this analysis (doc no: 16090/04). Two of the seven overall 'Objectives' are pertinent.

Objective 3 is 'to maximise capacity within European Union bodies and Member States to detect, investigate and prosecute terrorists and prevent attacks'. These measures include three measures already in the pipeline: i) a draft Council Decision on the exchange of information and cooperation concerning terrorist offences (Council doc no: 15871/04); ii) a draft Decision on the exchange of information extracted from the criminal record (Council doc no: 15281/04); iii) a draft Framework Decision on simplifying the exchange of information and intelligence between the law enforcement authorities of Member States particularly in respect of serious crimes including terrorist acts (original proposal from Sweden, doc on:10215/04) – this is referred to as introducing the 'principle of availability' as endorsed by the 'Hague Programme' (4.11.04). This 'Objective' contains no reference to the introduction of intelligence evidence in court proceedings nor of 'special investigative techniques'.[42]

Objective 6 'to address factors which contribute to support for, and recruitment into, terrorism' was added in the June 2004 version of the Action Plan (doc no: 10010/3/04, after 11 March bombings). The June and December Action Plans (2004) contain under this Objective:

> 'conduct more detailed studies, including academic studies, of recruitment to terrorism in specific contexts such as prisons, in schools, in universities or in mosques; studies into the role of the media, including the internet, in radicalisation or in promoting support or sympathy for terrorists...' (6.1.3)

Another point concerns investigating 'links between extreme religious or political beliefs ... and support for terrorism'. The December 2004 Action Plan now assigns this task to SitCen (the European Union's Situation Centre) to include relevant material in its 'assessments'.[43]

The concept of 'radicalisation and recruitment' is now widely used in European Union justice and home affairs documents.[44] The Action Plan notes that: 'countering radicalisation and recruitment needs a joint strategy of police and security services'. The first ever meeting of the Council's Counter Terrorism Group (CTG) and the Police Chiefs Task Force (PCTF) led to a report making recommendations 'to better structure the process of intelligence-gathering'.

A report on 'recruitment to terrorism' has been completed – though this is not public (6.1.1). However the *European Voice* newspaper reports (9.12.04) that a report drawn up after the discussions between the (CTG) and PCTF identifies mosques, the internet and prisons as 'hot spots' for the recruitment to 'extremists' by terrorist groups. It recommends that national security services should increase their intelligence-gathering at such locations and that Europol should undertake more 'profiling' of 'Islamic extremists'.

The role of the European Union's Counter-Terrorism Coordinator

Mr Gijs de Vries was appointed by the Council as the 'Counter-Terrorism Coordinator' after the bombings in Madrid on 11 March 2004. One of de Vries' jobs has been to conduct evaluation of 'national anti-terrorism arrangements' and to make 'recommendations' which 'may presuppose amendments or adjustments of existing legal or structural arrangements'.[45] The 'interim report' of the Coordinator (23 November 2004) makes a series of 'recommendations' and then 'additional suggestions' based on the evaluation reports. His second recommendation concerns the security services and 'information sharing':

> 'In order to detect, identify and facilitate profiling at a very early stage terrorists, terrorist networks and individuals supporting them as well as their plans and activities [there should be] access to law enforcement and other relevant administrative or government agencies databases (eg: police and border guards, social security, employment office) to cross information from various sources (data-mining) is crucial in particular in the course of the pre-investigative phase.'

The specific recommendation no 2 is that:

> 'Member States should have in place a procedure based on legislation/regulation allowing security services to have access to law enforcement and relevant government agencies/bodies' databases. This access would be strictly restricted to the need to know and should respect data protection requirements.'

Exactly how can 'data protection requirements' be respected when it is unlikely the individual(s) will know they are under surveillance unless they are later charged? For those not charged but 'caught up in the surveillance net', data protection is meaningless as they will not know their activities are being watched or how 'intelligence' gleaned is used or passed on.

Recommendation no. 3 deals directly with 'Intelligence as evidence in court' which sets out the 'need', recognises that this may affect fundamental rights, but does not deal with the consequences on the rights of defendants and the rule of law. The commentary opens by saying that:

> 'In most Member States intelligence information and in particular covertly obtained intelligence are not admissible as such for use in judicial proceedings.'

He recognises that security services are 'reluctant' for 'intelligence information' to be used in court because this could lead to the 'identification of sources' and the 'disclosure of certain special techniques'. A 'key point' is the:

> 'disclosure of information to the judge and the defence'

and could mean that the:

> 'security service members will have personally to testify in court as privileged witnesses in the framework of an open or closed session etc.'

It might be observed that there is a big difference for fundamental rights whether such evidence is heard in 'open or closed session', whether 'information' is disclosed to the defence lawyer and the defendant, and whether they are allowed to cross-examine.

For de Vries the issue is that 'intelligence' information means an 'enhanced capacity to reinforce criminal investigations and prosecutions.' This is all the more worrying as his philosophy set out in an earlier evaluation report refers to the need to:

> 'maximise the capacity to collect more and more pieces of intelligence' (doc no: 9876/04).

How might security services select instances to suit their purposes from these 'pieces of intelligence' to present to a court? Would a court be able to ask what other surveillance was carried out and what did it show?

He calls for the development of:

> 'a coherent set of laws and procedures to deal with the interaction of intelligence information and the judicial system while respecting fundamental human rights'.

In Recommendation no 3 de Vries says in view of the 'undoubtedly... positive impact' of using intelligence information in court, member states should take 'any necessary steps where needed'. As to fundamental rights he says that an 'evaluation' could:

> 'build on the current works in some Member States as well as in other fora (eg: the G8).'

In other words, the 'solution' found by 'some Member States' (eg: the United Kingdom) and 'G8' to balance the:

> 'civil rights of the individual and the rights and obligations of the state to protect citizens'

is a way of identifying 'best practices'.

Mr de Vries does not argue the case for the legalisation of 'special techniques' for intelligence gathering, he simply says that in some Member States there is 'appropriate legal basis' and under Recommendation 4 says:

> 'Member States should provide security services with appropriate legal basis for the use of special techniques for intelligence gathering.'

Here is no mention of protecting fundamental human rights – presumably because he does not think there is a problem. Recommendation 5 backs the focus on 'recruitment and radicalisation'. Recommendation no 6 is on 'suspect persons and potential perpetrators'. Information should be exchanged on:

> 'persons to be deported, suspect persons that have been trained and suspect persons travelling to or coming from sensitive regions.'

The concept of a 'suspect person' is not defined and can only be taken to mean a person who has 'come to the notice' of the security service or law enforcement agencies. To place under surveillance someone who is known to have been 'trained' to carry out terrorist acts is one thing, but people can be deported for many reasons quite unconnected with terrorism. Moreover, it might be asked: is a person a suspect if they attend a mosque where 'radical' views are expressed and who then travels to a 'sensitive region'?

Security services 'should deepen and widen the exchange of information' on suspect persons (and potential perpetrators) and, in the light of 'ongoing works within the G8', the European Union should continue to discuss how this exchange can be improved – whether within the European Union or with G8 countries is not clear.[46]

Recommendation no 7 refers to Europol's role in 'ongoing investigations' and the problem of the police having to get the permission of a prosecutor to pass over information. He proposes that an *ad hoc* working group be created to overcome 'obstacles'. Recognising that security services are reluctant to give information to Europol, he sees the establishment of 'a security service dimension within SitCen' as the solution.[47] Border controls and the new European Border Agency are another essential aspect of 'gathering and systematic intelligence sharing with law enforcement bodies and security services'.

Mr de Vries makes a number of 'suggestions' which include member states with a 'Muslim community' giving 'support to moderate Islam (and the promotion of intercultural dialogue) ... as a part of a national counter terrorism programme'.

Few of the Recommendations by de Vries are in the adopted Action Plan. However, part of his role is to put, or keep, major issues on the table. It is noteworthy that the Coordinator largely ignores the differences within the European Union member states in their replies to the questionnaire. Issues on which there is a determination within the General Secretariat (especially when backed by key member states and discussions in international fora) are often kept alive and then pushed through.

At an 'informal High Level European Union–United States Freedom, Security and Justice meeting' in Luxembourg on 13-14 January 2005 the 'treatment of classified information in criminal proceedings' was discussed.[48] ('High-Level' means a meeting of top officials from both sides). The 'Outcomes' of the meeting says that:

> 'The meeting addressed the difficulty of using security intelligence on alleged terrorists if the source of this intelligence cannot be disclosed in courts. The Presidency will invite Member States to answer as soon as possible the questionnaire drawn up in the G8 context. The United States offered to submit a paper outlining what the obstacles are and how they could be overcome. The European Union side will then consider the possibility of involving Eurojust and national policy-makers in a workshop on this issue, which is seen by the United States as vital for the credibility of counter-terrorism.'

The proposal first mooted in 2002 and now backed by the United States, United Kingdom, G8, European Union-United States Dromoland Declaration, and the

European Union's Counter Terrorism Coordinator is still very much on the agenda.

Council of Europe: Draft Convention

It is not surprising that these far-ranging developments are echoed in the Council of Europe (CoE, 45 member states). After 11 September 2001, the Council of Europe set up a Multidisciplinary Legal Group on International Action against Terrorism (GMT). Its final report, in November 2002, set out a number of priorities including research on the concepts of *'apologie du terrorisme'* and 'incitement to terrorism'. The research project was published on 24 June 2004.[49] It noted that whereas incitement to commit a criminal offence is common in the member states, *apologie* of a crime is not. The project used a questionnaire to compile an analysis of the law in the Council of Europe and defined *'apologie du terrorisme'* as:

'the public expression of praise, support or justification of terrorists and/or terrorist acts'.

Of the forty-five states only eight replies met the criteria that their national legislation defined *'apologie du terrorisme'* and/or 'incitement to terrorism' as a specific criminal offence – these were Bulgaria, Denmark, France, Hungary, Spain, United Kingdom, Italy and Switzerland. Only three states mentioned *'apologie du terrorisme'* as a specific crime – Denmark, France and Spain (Belgium said it intended to). A number of states raised the problem of free expression and freedom of the press if *'apologie du terrorisme'* were to become a crime.

In parallel, in February 2003, the Committee of Ministers set up an 'ad hoc Committee of Experts on Terrorism' with the acronym CODEXTER to implement the priorities of *'apologie du terrorisme'* and 'incitement to terrorism'. CODEXTER is working on a Draft Convention on the prevention of terrorism the latest version of which is dated 14 January 2005.[50] The scope is set out in Article 4.1 which says that:

'For the purpose of this Convention, "public provocation to commit an act of terrorism" means the distribution, or otherwise making publicly available, of a message to the public, with the intent to incite the commission of an act of terrorism, including where the message, although not directly advocating such acts, would be reasonably interpreted to have that effect, inter alia, by presenting an act of terrorism as necessary and justified'.

Article 4.2 says a criminal offence as defined in 4.1 should be adopted in domestic law when committed unlawfully and intentionally provided that: 'the provocation causes an imminent danger or likelihood of one or more terrorist acts being committed'. A footnote to Article 4.1 says:

'The CODEXTER considered a proposal to include the "terrorist motive" in Articles 4-6 as follows: which has the purpose by its nature or context to intimidate a population or to compel a government or an international organisation to do or abstain from doing any act. The CODEXTER will revert to this issue on second reading' (footnote 15 referring back to footnote 3).

Articles 4 and 5 cover recruitment and training for terrorism. Article 7 sets out 'ancillary offences' where it would be a criminal offence if a person 'participates as an accomplice' in Articles 4-6 or 'organises or directs others to commit an offence' under these Articles.

The European Union's Action Plan on terrorism (December 2004) records its support for this initiative which includes 'criminalisation of public provocation to commit acts of terrorism' (point 1.3.1). Although the European Union is taking part in CODEXTER, a meeting of Justice and Home Affairs Counsellors (experts on justice and home affairs based in the permanent representatives office of each member state in Brussels) in March recorded that 'the vast majority of delegations were sceptical as to a comprehensive convention against terrorism of the Council of Europe' and 'preferred to focus, at present, on the United Nations work in this field'[51]

However, as the year progressed the Netherlands Council Presidency and now that of Luxembourg is taking a more proactive approach by seeking to establish a European Union member states 'position' on a number of issues. A report from the Luxembourg Presidency at the end of January 2005 refers to discussions in the European Union's Multidisciplinary Group on Organised Crime (CODEXTER experts).[52] First, there appears to be a disagreement among member states on the inclusion of the United Nations Convention on the Suppression of the Financing of Terrorism. The Presidency is recommending keeping it in, while several member states are 'concerned' that:

> 'the inclusion of that convention would lead to a criminalisation of preparatory acts (e.g. public provocation) to a preparatory act (financing) to a preparatory act of the actual "act of terrorism". These Member States regard such a criminalisation as too far reaching.'

A later report, on 4 February, takes up the primary definition in Article 4.1.[53] A majority of European Union governments accept the definition as drafted. However, 'several delegations' wanted to delete the following words at the end: 'by presenting an act of terrorism as necessary and justified', which would be a definite improvement. The result of the discussion was a fudge. The majority position held subject to the addition of a new point 7 in the preamble: 'Recognising that this Convention is not intended to affect established principles relating to freedom of expression and freedom of association in national legal systems.'

Whereas the research study in 2004 showed only three European Union member states had a law akin to *apologie*, now the majority of them are in favour of such a law. Like the Council of Europe's Cyber Crime Convention this one is open to non-Council states to sign up to. During the latter stages of the discussions on the Cyber Crime Convention, the United States joined in and a number of highly retrogressive changes were made.

Conclusions and implications

As a result of the judgment in the United Kingdom House of Lords Court of Appeal on 16 December 2004 – which declared that indefinite detention without trial was unlawful – the United Kingdom government is to bring forward new legislation. This followed the appeal by 12 men held in Belmarsh high security prison in south

London and Woodhill prison under the Anti-Terrorism, Crime and Security Act 2001 (ATCSA 2001). Lord Hoffman, one of the nine judges, said that:

> 'The real threat to the life of the nation... comes not from terrorism but from laws such as these.'

The use of 'intelligence information' in court or in 'intelligence assessments' for issuing 'control orders'– against people for whom there is insufficient evidence to bring criminal charges – would bring fundamental changes to any normal concept of criminal justice systems in democracies. It could herald, as in the United Kingdom, vetted defence lawyers, refusal to let defendants know the evidence against them, *in camera* (closed) court session, the use of 'intelligence information' from third countries where it will be impossible to question the source, or whether the 'information' had been obtained as a result of torture or ill-treatment or 'rendition'.[54]

The demand for these changes needs to be seen in context. Since 11 September 2001 the European Union has adopted measures to introduce its own passenger name record scheme recording the movements of all third country nationals who enter as well as the external movements of European Union citizens; agreed on the introduction of biometric passports and a huge database carrying personal details; and is planning to introduce the mandatory retention by service providers of all communications traffic data. These measures have little to do with combating terrorism but together seek to make available to the law enforcement and security agencies a mass of personal data over which there are few, if any, controls as to its use.[55] In terms of tackling terrorism there will simply be a bigger and bigger 'haystack' in which to find the same number of 'needles'.

In addition there are new European Union proposals based on the so-called 'principle of availability' agreed under the European Union's 'Hague Programme' on justice and home affairs.[56] This means that if information on a person is held in one agency in a European Union member state, then it can be accessed by any other agency in any other member state. There is also another new 'principle' being put forward by the European Commissioner's Director-General, Mr Frattini, who says there is a need for a 'principle that information may be passed on with the prior consent of the party forwarding it'. This is to enable the passing of personal data to a third state such as the United States, and the 'prior consent' is not that of the individual concerned but the agency which gathered it. It is impossible to control who has access to data in, for example, the United States, which has over 1,500 agencies.[57] What may be a supposition or speculation about an individual's activities in one state may be added to or interpreted quite differently in another.

– *widening the net*

The Council of the European Union has reached 'political agreement' on a 'Council Decision on the exchange of information and cooperation concerning terrorist offences'. This envisages in Article 2.1 the exchange of 'information' during investigations and prosecutions concerning terrorist offences as set out in Article 1 to 3 of the 2002 Framework Decision on combating terrorism.[58] The 'information' is to be communicated to Europol and Eurojust (European Union prosecutors) and made *'accessible as soon as possible to the authorities of other interested Member States'*. It is sensible that such information should be made available. However, the proposal contains no provision for the 'information' to be removed/deleted should a person be found innocent. There is no provision for the 'information' passed over on those caught up in a 'criminal investigation' but never charged or convicted to be removed/deleted. This is especially worrying as an 'investigation' into a suspected terrorist offence would embrace not just the subject but their family, friends and work and social associates to see if there were any links to the suspected offence. A typical investigation could involve 20-40 other people who are found to be quite innocent but 'information' on them could be 'accessible' to dozens of agencies across the 25 European Union member states.

In April 2004, ten Muslim 'suspects' were arrested and held for questioning in the north of England but were never charged – this could have led to several hundred names and personal details being put into European Union-wide circulation, with no obligation for this data to be deleted. If there is no obligation to delete the names and details of innocent people, they could find themselves on 'watch-lists' for years to come.

There is another problem with the draft Decision. The intention is to widen the scope from those persons, groups and entities placed on updated lists of terrorist groups on formally adopted European Union lists to all those investigated under Articles 1 to 3 of the controversial Framework Decision on combating terrorism (2002) which, despite some amendment, is still ambiguous as to where the line is drawn between terrorism and large-scale protests. It covers, for example, those acting with the aim of:

> 'unduly compelling a Government or international organisation to perform or abstain from performing any act' (Art 1.ii)

To broaden the scope of cooperation on terrorism in this way opens the way for abuse and its application to non-terrorist offences.

– *the effects of gathering intelligence through 'special investigative techniques'*
Of direct relevance to the use of 'intelligence information' in courts is the legalisation of 'special investigative techniques' (eg: tapping and bugging), techniques the use of which in the past – because they are intrusive, covert and open to abuse – has been limited and very strictly controlled (usually requiring authorisation by a court).

From the 'security' perspective, measures and practices are being introduced to track peoples' movements, to data-mine public and commercial databases, retain and search all telecommunications, create 'watch-lists', infiltrate undercover agents in suspect groups and to recruit informers.[59] Undercover agents and informants inhabit a world of 'hearsay', manipulation and *agent-provocateurs*. Communities, mosques, individuals and groups are targeted for 'disruption' – people are stopped and searched, arrested and released without charge, bank accounts closed without explanation, mysterious burglaries occur, and dissension is encouraged by infiltrators to split and divide groups. Already the security agencies have gathered a mass of 'intelligence' and information on 'suspect' individuals and groups. Many groups and individuals are under 'suspicion' and under surveillance but very few so far have been charged with terrorist offences. In the next phase of the internal 'war on terrorism' the build-up of 'intelligence information' on 'suspected' individuals and groups and targeted communities in European Union states is going to expand enormously.

There are lessons from history when surveillance based on suspicion (rather than investigation leading to trial) becomes the norm. British Irish Rights Watch observed, when commenting on the United Kingdom Prevention of Terrorism Bill, that in Northern Ireland:

> 'Gathering and controlling intelligence took priority over the detection and prevention of crime. The need to recruit, and keep in place, informants meant that some agents were allowed to participate in crimes without being prosecuted, while others were granted *de facto* immunity in order not to blow agents' cover. As a result many people died needlessly in the name of saving lives.'[60]

The use of 'special investigative techniques' aided by undercover agents and informers 'hoovers' up 'intelligence' on specific 'targets' and everyone else who may unknowingly come into contact with them. Such methods carried out covertly and unaccountably (except to the agencies themselves) will lead to an unacceptable intrusion into social and political activity in a democratic society. The lives of the Muslim communities and those who go to mosques to worship become subject to an all pervasive and intrusive surveillance – which, though targeted at potential terrorists, soon extends to all suspected crimes and then to everyday activities.

These practices, techniques and changes in the legal process are, moreover, likely to spill over into the mainstream criminal justice system and establish new norms.[61]

The inexorable logic of the explosion in intelligence-gathering and targeting undertaken by a host of agencies across Europe is that the demands of the law enforcement and security agencies are going to grow for the detention or criminal prosecution of 'suspected' terrorists, 'sympathisers' and 'apologists'. Those who in previous times supported the North Vietnamese and the African National Congress and a host of liberation struggles in the 1960s and 1970s and those today, including the Palestinian struggle, are liable to be caught up in the surveillance 'net'.

Communities which house 'suspect communities' are targeted and subjected to intensive surveillance. Religious and political activity is infiltrated and spied on. And all this is based on the institutionalised racism of post 11 September 2001 –

a racism embedded in the 'politics of fear'.[62] Privacy, accountability, data protection, respect for fundamental rights and democratic norms disappear for those targeted or innocently caught up in the process.

Since 11 September 2001 governments, ministers and officials at all levels of the European Union have maintained that the swathe of new measures introduced have all been 'balanced' as between the needs of security and respect for fundamental rights. Concerned civil society groups across Europe know differently as do refugees, those stopped and searched and detained, and the communities subject to surveillance.[63]

In a democracy when the rights and freedoms of the few are curtailed so, too, are the rights and freedoms of us all.

References

1 In response to civil liberties critiques the previous Justice and Home Affairs Commissioner in the European Commission, Antonio Vittorino, said:
> 'We have not created emergency legislation, we did not create special courts, we did not create special regimes of detention. Those are the areas where real, serious limitations to civil liberties might arise' (launch of the 'Tampere II' process in July 2004).

2 http://www.statewatch.org/news/2005/mar/atcsa-2001-pt-4.htm

3 Privy Counsellors Review Committee: http://www.statewatch.org/news/2003/dec/16ukguantanamo.htm

4 'Counter-terrorism powers: reconciling security and liberty in an open society' (Cm 6147): http://www.statewatch.org/news/2004/feb/uk-CT-discussion-paper.pdf

5 On 21 July 2004 the parliamentary Joint Committee on Human Rights published a report on the 'option paper': http://www.statewatch.org/news/2004/aug/jt-hum-cttee-terr.htm.pdf and raised some of the issues in the Privy Counsellor Review Committee: Anti-terrorism, Crime and Security Act 2001 Review: http://www.statewatch.org/news/2003/dec/atcsReport.pdf

6 Judgment on ATCSA 2001, 16.12.04: http://www.statewatch.org/news/2004/dec/belmarsh-appeal.pdf

7 Statement by the Home Secretary on the introduction of control orders for terrorist 'suspects': http://www.statewatch.org/news/2005/jan/10uk-control-orders.htm

8 Statement on the use of intercepts as evidence: http://www.statewatch.org/news/2005/jan/11uk-intercepts-evidence.htm

9 UK: Egyptian national 'unlawfully detained' after intervention by Prime Minister: http://www.statewatch.org/news/2004/nov/03blair.htm

10 There appears to be some dispute over how many people could be served control orders. Charles Clarke, the Home Secretary, said that about one hundred could be affected but the Prime Minister says there are over two hundred people who are 'suspected' terrorists in the UK.

11 PTA 2005: http://www.statewatch.org/news/2005/mar/uk-pta-2005.pdf

12 One of the released Belmarsh detainees must under his bail conditions 'remain at all times' in his house, report in by phone five times a day, wear an electronic tag 'at all times', cannot allow anyone else into his house other than his family, lawyer, or 'other such person approved by the Home Office by prior appointment', no computers, mobile phones can be used in his house – which can be searched at any time.

13 Daily Telegraph, 28.1.05.

14 Ben Emmerson's Opinion: http://www.statewatch.org/news/2005/feb/opinion-on-pta-bill.pdf
15 Regulatory Assessment: http://www.statewatch.org/news/2005/mar/pt-bill-reg-assess.pdf
16 http://www.guardian.co.uk/print/0%2C3858%2C5155156-111274%2C00.html
17 He too confuses the issue of 'intercept evidence' and 'intelligence evidence'. The EU's Counter Terrorist Coordinator is on record as saying: 'In most Member States intelligence information and in particular covertly obtained intelligence are not admissible as such for use in judicial proceedings.' (November 2004)
18 In the Home Office statement on the interception of communications (deposited on 26.1.05) it says:
   'intercept evidence would be unlikely to assist in prosecuting terrorist targets and would not have made a critical difference in supporting criminal prosecution of those detained under ATCSA (Part 4) powers'
19 Court of Appeal, 11 August 2004: http://www.bailii.org/ew/cases/EWCA/Civ/2004/1123.html
20 Travel ban: http://www.guardian.co.uk/print/0,3858,5125522-111274,00.html and the testimony of one of the men: http://observer.guardian.co.uk/print/0,3858,5120738-102285,00.html
21 Statewatch: UK: Anti-terrorist stop & searches target Muslim communities: Report and analysis: http://www.statewatch.org/news/2004/jan/13uk-stop-and-search-targets-Muslim-communites.htm
22 G8 is comprised of the USA, Canada, France, Germany, Italy, the UK, Japan and Russia. The key G8 working groups are the Roma Group (set up in 1978 and comprised of intelligence and internal security officials, known as the Counter Terrorism Experts Group) the Lyon Group (law enforcement officials dealing with organised crime set up in June 1996) and the judicial cooperation group (there are others on issues like immigration).
23 The construction of terrorist lists advanced through the UN, USA and EU was accompanied by measures to track and freeze funding for suspected terrorist groups.
24 On Canada see: http://www.cbc.ca/story/canada/national/2004/12/10/security-certificate-041210.html
25 These were previously known as the 'Lyon Group Recommendations'.
26 EU combating terrorism or crime? http://www.statewatch.org/news/2004/jun/08eu-terrorism-and-crime.htm
27 See survey of current police powers: http://www.statewatch.org/news/2005/feb/01police-data-exchanges.htm
28 'Controlled deliveries' is a relatively recent development and describes a police or customs operation which is deliberately set up by the agencies in order to catch perpetrators.
29 On 25 June 2003 the EU and USA signed agreements on extradition and mutual legal assistance – these have yet to be ratified by the USA and a number of EU member states. The agreement on mutual legal assistance includes the creation of joint investigation teams and requests for 'assistance' – for example, to place under surveillance an individual or group and supply the 'products' of this to the requesting state. See: http://www.statewatch.org/news/2003/apr/01Auseuag.htm
30 Although the UK was not represented at the Dublin meeting, Home Office, police, MI5 and MI6 officials were at the earlier key meetings in G8 of the Roma and Lyon groups. These officials, together with their counterparts from three other EU states (France,

Germany and Italy), had by the time of the meeting on 23 February already agreed on the 'concerns', sent out a questionnaire and received replies from all G8 members (including from the UK).

31 EU doc no 6862/04: http://www.statewatch.org/news/2005/jan/6862-eu-us.pdf
32 'Special investigative techniques: http://www.statewatch.org/news/2004/may/G8justice04-legal3.pdf
33 'enhancing the legal framework': http://www.statewatch.org/news/2004/may/G8justice04-legal2.pdf
34 'protecting intelligence': http://www.statewatch.org/news/2004/may/G8justice04-legal4.pdf
35 See, Observer, 19.12.04, article by Martin Bright. It is alleged that one of the men held in Belmarsh prison did exactly this.
36 See, http://www.statewatch.org/news/2004/feb/09gp-guardian.htm
37 Dromoland Declaration: http://www.statewatch.org/news/2005/jan/dromoland-10809.pdf
38 Questionnaire on prevention of terrorism: http://www.statewatch.org/news/2005/jan/eu-g8-10694.pdf
39 It should be noted that the EU-US agreements on extradition and mutual assistance have not yet been formally adopted by the USA. However, such 'mutual cooperation' can take place under existing bilateral agreements.
40 Responses to the questionnaire: http://www.statewatch.org/news/2005/feb/terr-quest-12041.04.pdf
41 A related issue to the use of intelligence in court proceedings is that of freezing or seizing the bank accounts of individuals and groups on terrorist lists. This raises problems when it is used as a 'preventive measure' which has 'led to a series of legal questions' (Council doc no: 14180/3/04):

> 'These questions range from the criteria which should be applied and the evidence which is needed for administrative freezing, the relation of administrative freezing to judicial freezing, seizure and confiscation, to matters of due process, availability of de-listing procedures and the role of intelligence in the designation process.'

42 Though a reference to the possibility of 'the adoption of legislation for the use of special techniques for intelligence gathering' was slipped into a Presidency Briefing Note given to the press at the Summit.
43 Solana statement: http://www.statewatch.org/news/2004/jun/solana-jha-june-04.pdf See also: Statewatch article: http://www.statewatch.org/news/2005/jan/06sitcen.htm
44 See for example Council doc no: 5670/04, dated 6.2.04, which refers to this concept and gathering details on 'motives for radicalisation within the EU'. The document also suggests looking at 'the Richard Reid/shoe bomb case' and the 'ricin plot in the UK' (which never existed).
45 Council doc no: 14306/3/04: http://www.statewatch.org/news/2005/jan/14306-re03.04-vries.pdf
46 This may be related to discussions with the USA on creating common 'watchlists' or 'red watchlists'.
47 Emergence of SitCen: http://www.statewatch.org/news/2005/jan/06sitcen.htm
48 Informal High-Level EU-US meeting: http://www.statewatch.org/news/2005/feb/eu-us-jan-05-5437.pdf
49 'Apologie du terrorisme' and 'incitement to terrorism': Analytical report: http://www.statewatch.org/news/2005/jan/ribbelink.pdf